21ˢᵗ
Century
Skills Library

ROAD TO RECOVERY
AMERICAN BISON

Barbara A. Somervill

Cherry Lake Publishing
Ann Arbor, Michigan

CHERRY LAKE Publishing

Published in the United States of America by Cherry Lake Publishing
Ann Arbor, MI
www.cherrylakepublishing.com

Content Adviser: Dr. Cormack Gates, Co-Chair (North America) IUCN (International Union for the Conservation of Nature and Natural Resources) Bison Specialist Group; Coordinator, Environmental Science Program, Faculty of Environmental Design, University of Calgary, Calgary, Alberta, Canada

Photo Credits: Page 19, Photo courtesy of Library of Congress; page 22, © Raymond Gehman/Corbis

Map by XNR Productions, Inc.

Library of Congress Cataloging-in-Publication Data
Somervill, Barbara A.
  American bison / by Barbara A. Somervill.
     p. cm.
  Includes index.
  ISBN-13: 978-1-60279-031-5 (hardcover)
  ISBN-10: 1-60279-031-0 (hardcover)
  1. American bison—Juvenile literature. 2. Endangered species—Juvenile literature. I. Title.
  QL737.U53S665 2008
  599.64'3—dc22   2007003871

*Cherry Lake Publishing would like to acknowledge the work of
The Partnership for 21st Century Skills.
Please visit www.21stcenturyskills.org for more information.*

TABLE OF CONTENTS

CHAPTER ONE

ROUNDUP!

It is an early, frosty October morning. Horses snort and stamp, anxious to be on their way. Local ranchers, park employees, and veterinarians are about to start four days of demanding work. The bison roundup will soon be under way at Badlands National Park in South Dakota.

A single plains bison grazes in South Dakota's Badlands National Park.

The park is a maze of deep canyons, rugged mountains, and multicolored ribbons of soil. Ridges, mounds, valleys, and curving streambeds carve the stark, beautiful landscape. The park's mixed-grass prairie is ideal for plains bison. And this is what the roundup is all about—bison.

Although this is a natural home for plains bison, they have not lived in this area continuously. Plans were made to reintroduce bison here in the 1960s. In 1963, four animal species arrived at Badlands to "repopulate" the park: black-footed ferrets, bighorn sheep, swift foxes, and American bison. The experiment was a remarkable success. Today, more than 1,000 bison live in the park, and they continue to produce healthy young. However, the park can support only so many bison. Now some need to be captured and relocated.

In a narrow canyon, a half dozen bison browse on tufts of grass. Bison

thrive on native grasses and sedges. As the cowboys approach on horseback,

the bison snort and stamp. They cluster together. Then, as the horses edge

Bison eat a variety of prairie grasses.

around them, the bison stampede toward the canyon's entrance. The cowboys herd the bison into pens and through narrow passages, where the veterinarians can examine them closely. Watch it! Those horns are sharp, and the bison don't particularly enjoy the process.

This roundup brings 657 bison in for medical exams and shots for various diseases. The veterinarians also draw blood to determine each animal's **genetic** makeup. Today, there are very few 100 percent pure bison. Most bison are a mix of bison and cattle. Maintaining herds of purebred bison is important for keeping the bison species healthy.

After the roundup, the park makes arrangements to ship 278 of these animals to six different states and several different Native American tribes. The bison will join herds belonging to the Oglala Sioux and the Santee Sioux, among others.

The process of cutting out specific animals from a herd is called culling, and culling is necessary to keep herds healthy. A well-managed herd, even one that lives wild, needs to have a balance of males and females and a mix of ages. The 2006 bison roundup helped to balance the Badlands herd. It also provided a mix of healthy beasts to fill other herds on **reservations** in the prairie states.

CHAPTER TWO

THE STORY OF AMERICAN BISON

Shaggy, dense, dark coats keep the bison warm in the coldest weather.

The thick fur lies like a cape around the head, neck, hump, and front legs.

Bison shed their coats for the summer, and a thinner, light brown coat

takes its place. The summer coat keeps the animal cool while its twitchy

flyswatter of a tail bats away annoying flies and gnats.

A bison's thick, wooly coat serves as a barrier against the elements.

At their largest, bison stand 6 feet (1.8 meters) tall and measure 10 feet (3 m) long. The males are one-third larger than females, but both are sizable, weighing between 1,000 and 2,000 pounds (454 and

Thick, sharp horns are the bison's main weapon against attacks by wolves or bears.

10

907 kilograms). A bison usually has a broad chest, a thick neck, and short, stubby legs.

Both males and females have short, black, curved horns. The horns are an excellent weapon against attack. The horns are made

North American bison and European bison are close relatives. This European bison lives in a zoo.

from the same material as our fingernails—keratin.

Bison are members of the bovine, or cow, family. They are distant relatives of Asia's water buffalo and Africa's cape buffalo. Their closest relatives are wisents, or European bison. Most bison live in captive herds.

Bison calves depend on their mothers for the first year of life.

In the wild, bison gather together in small herds of from four to 50

animals. Herds mainly consist of females, their calves, and juveniles of

both sexes. Bulls live separately, except during mating season.

When summer comes, the males rejoin the herds and put on quite a show. They roar and snort and tear up the earth with their paws. They roll and rip up the grass and challenge other males to gain the rights to mate with the herd females. The bulls face each other head-on, stamping their feet. A smaller bull usually backs down, but if not, the two butt heads in a dangerous shoving match until one retreats. The two competitors also use their horns, ripping at the other's head and neck. The winner mates with females and also stands guard to make sure no other males try to mate with his cows.

The females carry their calves for nine and a half months. A newborn calf weighs about 66 pounds (30 kg) and nurses as soon as it can. Within just a few hours, the infant calf can stand up and run with the rest of the herd. Newborns are orange-brown at birth and begin growing brown

adult fur at about two months old. Calves grow remarkably quickly drinking mothers' milk. At seven months, calves stop drinking milk and live on a diet of grasses, sedges, and other plants.

At one year, a healthy calf may weigh more than 400 pounds (181 kg). By three years old, the females are old enough to bear young. Males in the wild can first father calves when they are about five or six years old. In the wild, a bison can expect to live 12 to 20 years. In the safety of a zoo, they may live as long as 40 years.

CHAPTER THREE

ENDANGERED!

Herds of bison have been around for hundreds of thousands of years in North America.

At least 200,000 years ago, the animals we call bison crossed into North

America over the Bering land bridge from Asia. Glaciers prevented them

from moving southward until 120,000 years ago. They adapted to the

Bison are a keystone species of the prairie. Both animals and plants need bison to survive. The bison feed on various grasses and sedges and leave droppings on prairie land. Seeds in the droppings send out shoots that spread plant species to new locations. The droppings fertilize the soil, encouraging more plant growth.

Prairie dogs thrive in areas where the bison live. They depend on bison to keep grasses cropped low, which allow the prairie dogs to see predators approaching. Flies and dung beetles use bison droppings as nurseries for their young. A natural increase in insect populations follows, which in turn draws insect eaters, including birds, prairie dogs, and reptiles.

Larger predators, such as wolves, mountain lions, and coyotes, feed on the small prairie critters as well as sick, injured, elderly, or young bison. Even in death, bison help the prairie. A dead bison feeds vultures, crows, and other animals. Insects eat the meat. Slowly, the body decays, and the nutrients in bones and flesh feed the soil.

Now, think of an animal in your area. Think of what it eats, where it lives, and what eats it. How do you think this animal affects other living creatures—including yourself?

vast sea of grasses that filled the Great Plains. Another cold spell lasting 100,000 years prevented people from occupying the continent. Finally, about 14,000 years ago, the glaciers receded. Clans that hunted and gathered food from the wild traveled to hunt the bison just as they did other large creatures.

As these clans evolved into tribes, those tribes continued

to hunt bison. They hunted on foot, chasing the bison over cliffs. The practice and the cliffs became known as buffalo jumps. Small herds stampeded over the buffalo jumps to their deaths.

A glut of meat meant bison roasts and stews while the meat was fresh. Then the tribes made **pemmican** by drying the meat, pounding it fine, and mixing it with melted fat to preserve it. The people used the skins for clothes, shoes, and dwellings. They used other parts of the body for sewing thread and bowstrings. Dried bison dung became fuel for campfires, and hooves were boiled down to make glue.

When Europeans began exploring the southern Great Plains, they did so on horseback. For native people, horses were a novelty. Once the native people acquired horses, it changed the way they hunted. Hunters rode beside the herds, hunting with bows and arrows.

The bison population had expanded, and by the early 1800s, between 30 million and 60 million roamed free on the plains. "The Indian was frugal in the midst of plenty. When the buffalo roamed the plains in multitudes, he slaughtered only what he could eat and of these he used to the hair and bones," said Luther Standing Bear, an Oglala Sioux author.

In the 1800s, the westward expansion of the United States endangered the American bison. When settlers began turning open prairie into farmland, bison herds and Plains Indians were in the way. As railroads laid tracks connecting east and west, bison and Indians were, again, in the way.

Some people thought if the bison were gone, the Plains Indians would also go. The Indians depended on the bison for food, and with no food source, tribes would have to leave the plains. That would make more land available to white settlers.

Getting rid of the bison became an organized business. Crews of

hunters, rifle loaders, blacksmiths, skinners, and cooks became efficient

killing machines.

Hunters shot as many bison as they possibly could. At $3 per hide

for average skins and $50 for each quality winter coat, money added up

In the 19th century, North American bison populations suffered
at the hands of hunters and others looking to make a profit.

quickly. Considering that the average worker earned about $1 per day in the mid-1800s, the pay for killing bison was tremendous. One hunter claimed to have killed 20,000 animals. Companies recorded slaughters of 2,000 to 100,000 beasts a day. Skinners stripped the skins from the animals; the meat rotted where it lay. Skins were used to make belts for machines, robes, and blankets.

From 1830 to 1890, the bison population on the North American plains went from more than 60 million animals to fewer than 1,000. William T. Hornaday, superintendent of the National Zoo in 1889, said, "The wild buffalo is practically gone forever, and in a few more years . . . nothing will remain of him save his old, well-worn trails along the watercourses." An entire species had nearly died out.

CHAPTER FOUR

THE ROAD TO RECOVERY

Bison have been on the road to recovery for more than 100 years. The loss

of so many beasts was quick and dramatic. Yellow Hand, a Cheyenne chief,

described the loss: "Yesterday, the buffalo was many as the blades of grass

upon the prairie. Today, the buffalo is few as the leaves on an oak tree in

Yellowstone National Park is a scenic refuge for today's plains bison.

winter." The time to save the bison species came when only 1,000 still lived

in the wild.

In 1899, James "Scotty" Philip purchased a small herd of five bison in

South Dakota. By the time he died in 1911, his herd had grown to nearly

1,000 beasts—a first step on the road to recovery.

Many of the world's wood bison live in Wood Buffalo National
Park in Alberta, Canada's largest national park.

A small herd survived on the protected lands of Yellowstone National Park. Twenty-one plains bison thrived in the park's Pelican Valley. It is the only continuous wild plains bison herd in North America.

In 1905, a group of conservationists met at New York City's Bronx Zoo to discuss ways of preserving the American bison. This group, the American Bison Society, intended to restock bison refuges in Oklahoma, Montana, South Dakota, and Nebraska. Two years later, 15 bison were loaded onto railroad cars on their way to Oklahoma's Wichita Mountain Preserve. These beasts formed a starter herd that now numbers 550.

Plains bison populations have expanded in public preserves and on private ranches. Wood bison population numbers have remained lower. Related to the plains bison, the wood bison is heavier, has a different build, and lives in far northern climates. Plans are under way to introduce to

Alaska a herd of wood bison from Canada. Building

a new herd there would help ensure the survival of

wood bison. In addition, this herd would enhance

Alaska's already extensive wildlife resources.

Currently, 40 percent of all wood bison

live in Alberta's Wood Buffalo National Park.

Unfortunately, many are infected with two serious

cattle diseases: bovine tuberculosis and brucellosis.

Tuberculosis affects the lungs and weakens the

animals. Brucellosis causes cows to miscarry calves,

give birth too early, or produce weak calves. The new

herd in Alaska would be stocked only with healthy,

disease-free wood bison.

CHAPTER FIVE

AMERICAN BISON TODAY

In 2004, U.S. senators Mike Enzi of Wyoming and Ben Nighthorse

Campbell of Colorado announced the reissuing of the buffalo nickel in

honor of the American bison. "The amazing feat of restoring a species that

dwindled to less than 1,000 in the 19th century is an achievement that

needs to be commemorated.

Their numbers stand at more

than 500,000 strong today,"

said Enzi.

Recently, conservationists

met in Denver, Colorado,

to discuss the future of the

The buffalo nickel pays tribute to the American bison for its important role in the history of the United States.

bison in North America. Interested groups included bison ranchers, Native American tribes in the Intertribal Bison Cooperative, the World Wildlife Fund (WWF), the World Conservation Union Bison Specialist Group, and the Nature Conservancy. These groups recognize that saving bison also means helping endangered black-footed ferrets, swift foxes, and Utah prairie dogs.

Today, only a half dozen genetically pure herds of plains bison exist. Most herds have bison with some cattle genes. Wild herds exist in several national parks: Yellowstone, Wind Cave, Henry Mountains, and Wood Buffalo. Yellowstone's wild herd is the largest and oldest plains bison herd. Yellowstone's Pelican Valley is home to 4,000 to 5,000 bison. About 600 to 700 calves are born each year.

Many restored herds trace their success back to the Bronx Zoo. For several years, the American Bison Society and the zoo shipped animals

Groups throughout North America are working together to protect and restore the bison.

west to add to herds on refuges and preserves in

western prairie states. Starter herds, protected on

private ranches and in national parks, flourished.

Life & Career Skills

In 1991, members of 19 tribes met in the sacred Black Hills of South Dakota. The purpose of the meeting was to unite toward a common mission: restoring bison to Indian nations in a way that matches native beliefs and practices. The goal of this collaboration was to establish or expand bison herds on reservation lands. Today, the Intertribal Bison Cooperative consists of 42 tribes with a combined bison herd of 8,000 animals.

In May 2006, five wild bison cows gave birth on the plains of eastern Montana. These calves were born in the new reserve founded by the American Prairie Foundation and the WWF. They were the first American bison calves born in this historic bison range in more than 100 years.

Today, more than 95 percent of American bison live on ranches. Truly wild bison need a place to roam, and until open prairie is restored, wild plains bison will continue to be threatened. We will never see herds in the millions again. But with careful management, thousands of bison will run wild on the same plains the first herds once roamed.

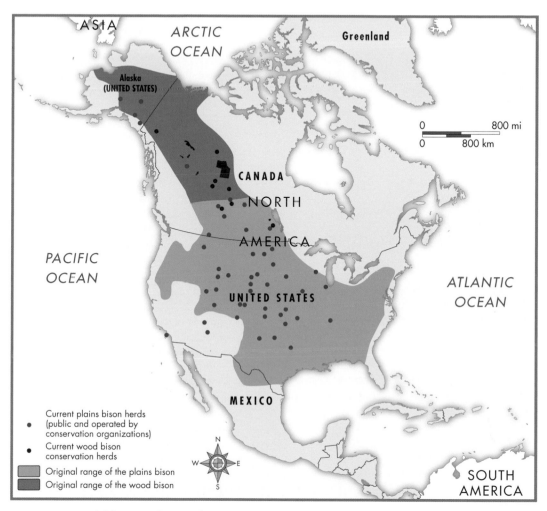

Map labels:

ASIA

ARCTIC OCEAN

Greenland

Alaska (UNITED STATES)

CANADA

NORTH AMERICA

PACIFIC OCEAN

UNITED STATES

ATLANTIC OCEAN

MEXICO

SOUTH AMERICA

0   800 mi
0   800 km

• Current plains bison herds (public and operated by conservation organizations)
• Current wood bison conservation herds
  Original range of the plains bison
  Original range of the wood bison

N W E S

This map shows where American bison—plains bison and wood bison—live in North America as well as where they lived in the past.

Glossary

bovine (BO-vyne) relating to or belonging to the animal family that includes cattle and bison

brucellosis (bruh-suh-LOW-siss) a disease that causes animals to miscarry their young or produce weak or premature young

conservationists (kon-sur-VAY-shun-ists) people who work to preserve environments, animals, or plants

genetic (jih-NEH-tik) involving the characteristics passed from parents to their young through genes

juveniles (JOO-vuh-nylz) the young of a species

keratin (CARE-uh-tin) a substance that is the protein base in producing hair, nails, feathers, and hooves

keystone species (KEE-stone SPEE-sheez) an animal or plant that many other animals and plants depend on for survival

pemmican (PEM-ih-can) meat that has been dried, pounded to a fine texture, and mixed with fat to preserve it

reservations (rez-uhr-VA-shunz) areas of land set aside for a particular purpose, such as a home for a Native American tribe

sedges (sej-iz) grasslike plants

species (SPEE-sheez) a group of similar animals or plants

tuberculosis (tuh-burk-yoo-LO-sis) a disease that causes infections in the lungs and complicates breathing

veterinarians (vet-uhr-uh-NAR-ee-unz) doctors that specialize in caring for animals

FOR MORE INFORMATION

Books

Kite, L. Patricia. *Watching Bison in North America.* Chicago: Heinemann Library, 2006.

Marrin, Albert. *Saving the Buffalo.* New York: Scholastic, 2006.

Patent, Dorothy Hinshaw. *The Buffalo and the Indians: A Shared Destiny.* New York: Clarion Books, 2006.

Picton, Harold. *Buffalo: Natural History and Conservation.* Stillwater, MN: Voyageur Press, 2005.

Waldman, Neil. *They Came from the Bronx: How the Buffalo Were Saved from Extinction.* Honesdale, PA: Boyds Mills Press, 2001.

Web Sites

National Parks Conservation Association—American Bison
www.npca.org/wildlife_protection/wildlife_facts/bison.html
For information on bison found in national parks

NatureWorks—American Bison
www.nhptv.org/natureworks/americanbison.htm
For photos and information on bison behavior

Wind Cave National Park—American Bison
www.nps.gov/wica/bison.htm
To find facts about the bison at the Wind Cave National Park

INDEX

ABOUT THE AUTHOR

Barbara A. Somervill writes children's nonfiction books on a variety of topics. She is particularly interested in nature and foreign countries. Somervill believes that researching new and different topics makes writing every book an adventure. When she is not writing, Somervill is an avid reader and plays bridge.